Blueprint of Business

The complete guide for entrepreneurs to create successful, risk-free & profitable business model.

By Ng Chin Siang

Contents

Chapter 1 Getting to know yourself 1
    Understand your internal motivation 3
    Turn your passion as your business.. 5
    Develop your habit as an entrepreneur 8
    Start small & safe.. 11

Chapter 2 Crafting strategy -Purpose of establishment 15
    Mission and Vision... 15
    Key Activities 17
    Key resources 21
    Key partners 23

Chapter 3 -Value Proposition 26
    Modern Elements of Value Propositions............................. 26
        Utility 26
        The New Economy.. 27
        Branding using Corporate Social Responsibility (CSR)....... 36
        Scarcity 37
        Cultural elements 39
    The framework of Value Proposition 41

Chapter 4 -Customer 43
    Customer Segmentation.. 43
        Geographic segmentation 45
        Demographic segmentation 45
        Psychographic segmentation 46
        Behavioral Segmentation 48

Customer Relationship 51

Chapter 5 Channels 54

Channel Strategy 54

Direct Channel 56

    Brick and click model 56

    Dropship model 57

    Omnichannel 58

Indirect channels-Distribution Partners 59

    Value-added sellers 59

    Wholesaler 61

    Licensing 62

    Franchising 63

    Original equipment manufacturers (OEM) 65

    Managed service provider (MSP) 66

    Systems integrators (SI) 67

    Independent software vendor (ISV) 68

    Affinity Marketing Partnership 70

    Sponsorship Marketing Partnership 71

    Affiliate Marketing Partnership 71

Partner Relationship Management 72

Chapter 6- Revenues 75

Revenues 75

    Asset sale 75

    Service Revenue 80

    Subscription 81

    Lending 84

    Renting 86

  Leasing 90

  Broker 93

  Licensing 97

  Advertising.. 99

 Revenue Management 102

  Acquiring the new customer 104

  Retaining existing customer 107

  Increasing the transaction value 110

  Optimizing prices 115

Chapter 7- Cost 118

 Financial Cost.. 118

  Operating expenses (OPEX) 119

  Capital Expenditures (CAPEX) 119

 Economic Cost 121

  Fixed Costs 121

  Variable Costs 122

  Sunk Cost 123

  Opportunity Cost 123

  The formula for Calculating Opportunity Cost 124

  Economies of Scale 128

  Economies of Scope... 130

 Cost Control & Performance Management........................ 133

  Budgetary control 135

  Horizontal analysis... 136

  Vertical analysis 139

Chapter 1 Getting to know yourself

Do you know who you are? Knowing yourself is the process of understanding yourself on the deeper level. As an adult, we act like everyone else and feeling insecure about it. It makes you think of the way of accomplishing your dream following your own destiny. Knowing yourself means to honor your values and belief, personality, moods, habits, body, and relationships with others. It means to accept your personalities such as strengths and weaknesses, passions and fears, likes and dislikes, desires and dreams. Try this link for free personality test:

https://www.personalityperfect.com/test/free-personality-test/
http://www.humanmetrics.com/personality/career-choices

It is necessary to take these tests as a guiding principle to make an informed decision on your career choice. Understand how you work best under different conditions. Your hopes and dreams create the pathway of your future. They help you establish the life you can be proud of living. Your dreams matter. It is worth going after it. Don't believe in anything less. Never settle for anything less.

If you want to become an entrepreneur, ask yourself:
What is your passion?
How do you turn your passion as your career?
How much is the capital requirement?
What products or services you provide?
What is your cost?
Who is your customer?
How to serve your customer?
How to create value for your customer?
How to sustain your business?
What are the support activities needed to create value for your customer?

And on and on until you know everything about your idea. Invest the time on your business idea, make it as your daily routine and work on it. It is the only way to realize your dream and unleash your full potential.

Understand your internal motivation

The most important thing for an entrepreneur is passion. As the life of an entrepreneur is tough, you need to work long hours and 24/7 for your own business. Finding the industry, you love is important for you to work diligently, even with no monetary reward. Passion is a form of intrinsic motivation. It is what you feel motivated to do it even with no external rewards; you enjoy the activity or take it as a chance to learn and actualize your full potential.

Intrinsic motivation creates positive emotion within yourself. When was the last time you did something for enjoyment? There are several activities you can do in leisure time. For instance, you may take a photo, plant a garden, play a sport, write a story, or read a book. These activities you enjoy, create positive feelings when it gives the sense of meaning in your life. It may also give you a sense of progress when you see that your effort is accomplishing something beneficial or competence when you learn something new or become more skilled.

Consider your motivation for reading this book. If you are reading it because you want to be gain knowledge on how to be a successful entrepreneur, you are acting based on intrinsic motivation. However, if you are reading it because you want to get rich, then you're driven by extrinsic motivation. For the third scenario, some of you may be in the situation of both. Success comes a long way, if you are not getting any reward, chances of quitting halfway are high. So, make sure you are more internally driven to be an entrepreneur. In simple words, find an activity that makes you feel happy to do it and expecting nothing in return in the initial stage of the business venture.

Turn your passion as your business

For those of you lack of idea on what to do, try to find any activity or hobby you enjoy the most. From there, start a business related to your interest. Other than business-related knowledge, you may need to master the domain knowledge of your business. For Example, if you would like to be a professional photographer, there's more than taking photographs. You may need to know how to start your own photo studio as a business. You must master all the other activities of your studio.

Are you skilled in exposure and lighting? Do you understand the needs for various lenses and focal length for a different shooting scene?
Are you able to find a customer that like your photography style and willing to pay for your professional service?
Have you looked what your competitors offer in the market?
Where will you operate your business?

    Even though there's always room for improvement, it's important for an entrepreneur to master the core activity of a business. You must be skillful on the domain knowledge, so gain relevant training to make the product or service marketable. Build skills at no cost. Take online courses for free from top-notch universities at edX & Coursera websites. Access the content for free and pay only for the certificate. On the other hands, try free or paid courses from

Udemy. You may find skill-based courses from Udemy.

https://www.edx.org/
https://www.coursera.org/
https://www.udemy.com/

    If you lack the skills or training, get it without cost wherever possible. Try to negotiate with education institutions or companies to train you in exchange for services rendered. Take a paid job or an internship. Look for hands-on experience from friends, family, and skilled acquaintances. If you choose the formal education, prepare around 5 to 6 figures budget. Public university costs lesser than the private one. You should maintain a consistent source of income while you're studying -if you need to go back to school for your skill development over a long period, so prepare with enough money for the living expenses too.

Once you have decided on what business will you offer, you need to treat it seriously. Even though your business is your passion, it doesn't mean it is only a weekend activity. It means being accountable for your passion and working on it daily. Instead of setting one unachievable goal, you may subdivide the big goal into smaller attainable tasks. In this way, working to achieve all the small goals help you realize your ultimate goal.

Develop your habit as an entrepreneur

If you are keeping your day job, decide that you will allocate your everyday schedule for the side hustle. For example, allocate time after dinner to develop your business, stick to the schedule until it becomes a part of the day after day activity. Don't make excuses during the habit formation stage. Stick to your timetable for

21 days. It helps to shape the good habit with these consistent efforts.

Keep telling yourself that you will become a successful entrepreneur. Visualize yourself as a sought-after entrepreneur as if you are already one, the more you imagine yourself to be one, the faster it accepts by your subconscious mind. You will act with confidence to achieve your dream.

Your social circle plays a big role in shaping your new role as an entrepreneur. Inform your family and friends you will be an entrepreneur. You will become more determined and motivated when you know others are motivating you to follow through your resolution. Create a new social circle with people with the same mindset. Join the activity you find interesting to mingle with others. Where can you find these supportive resources? Here are a few places to get you started:
https://www.startupgrind.com/

https://www.meetup.com/
https://freelancetofreedomproject.com/

It is important to find a balance between work and life. To be productive all the time, stick to 50/10 rule. Work non-stop for 50 minutes and rest for 10 minutes. It helps you to stay in focus without feeling tired. Give yourself a treat if you achieve the milestones of your progress. Each time when you reward yourself, you reaffirm and reinforce your behavior. Soon, you will associate unconsciously this positive result with the effort. As a result, it motivates you to become a successful entrepreneur.

Keep practicing your daily routine as an entrepreneur, don't give up easily. Be flexible enough to make changes if you're facing any difficulties. Change is the only constant thing in this world. Just be bold to embrace new ideas and face challenges along the journey.

Start small & safe

It's important to keep your current job. By keeping a reliable source of income, you don't have to worry about financial obligations. Ideally, when you start a business, try to change the role gradually from an employee to a consultant or part-time worker. It takes some time before you can make a living with a business. Furthermore, by keeping the day job is a safer path than venture into your own full-time business that hasn't produced any income yet. If you plan to start a business soon, avoid signing an employment contract with a restrictive clause, that inhibits you from pursuing the second source of income. Consider going through contract details with a lawyer.

Establishing a new business often needs a large sum of money. Use the available resources as much as you can. For instance, use a personal car for the business trip, use the garage as a workshop for products. If you have a home use it as the office or rent a co-working space with small rent. It saves a lot of money on office rent and related expenses.

In some point in your business, you may require a substantial amount of money to run a business. When you plan to get your funding, try to get your money from a close relative and friend. Negotiate the best term like low-interest rate, and a long repayment period; specify the loan terms in writing with clause specify if the business fails, you can pay back over a longer period. Other than that, propose the profit-sharing deals with them with no monthly payback commitment, or pay only when your business generated enough cash flow.

Find the potential angel investors or venture capitalist for funding your startup. However, if you can't get any money from them, try to get on-line financing. You may advertise the startup idea online and raise fund via a cloud-sourcing site like Kickstarter. https://www.kickstarter.com/start?ref=learn_top Pitch your project online to the public at large, if they like your idea, they will contribute collective fund to your project.

Settle the monthly commitment on time, pay the mortgage, student loan, car loan, credit card bill and any loan according to schedule. It is important to maintain a good personal credit score. Only apply for an additional loan when you can afford to repay. The consistent repayment history and low debt to income ratio are the main considerations for bank approving your loan. For the interest-free fund, try to make good use on the bank 0% credit transfer of your credit card balance, apply when you can pay the monthly installment.

For a business loan with an interest rate, take the loan only when you can repay with the consistent income. Choose non-collateral loan over the collateral loan, so you don't have to sell personal assets when you can't pay the loan. For a collateral loan, take it when you have none other credit options left and register business entity under limited liability form. A limited liability company (LLC) is a corporate structure whereby the company owner is not personally liable for the company's debts or liabilities. In simple words, the lender can claim only company assets if the company owner defaults on the loan payment.

Chapter 2 Crafting strategy -Purpose of establishment

As the founder of the company, an entrepreneur must be clear about the direction and roadmap of the company. The vision and mission guide every activity in the business. It is the grand strategy that defines a company. Thus, these statements should deliver a simple and concise message to everyone in the company. It should be memorable to stick on people's mind and complex enough to deliver the purpose of the establishment.

Mission and Vision

Mission statements emphasize current business activities. It defines the role of the company plays in the marketplace. Vision statements focus a company's future endeavors, target markets, technologies, or objectives that support the mission of a company. Values are the core beliefs of an organization. It is the guiding ethical principles that dictate how people behave in achieving the business goal.

Example: Coca-Cola
Mission
To refresh the world
To inspire moments of optimism and happiness
To create value and make a difference.

Vision
People: Be a great place to work where people are inspired to be the best they can be.
Portfolio: Bring to the world a portfolio of quality beverage brands that anticipate and satisfy people's desires and needs.
Partners: Nurture a winning network of customers and suppliers, together we create mutual, enduring value.

Planet: Be a responsible citizen that makes a difference by helping build and support sustainable communities.
Profit: Maximize long-term return to shareowner while being mindful of our overall responsibilities.
Productivity: Be a highly effective, lean and fast-moving organization

Values
Leadership: The courage to shape a better future
Collaboration: Leverage collective genius
Integrity: Be real
Accountability: If it is to be, it's up to me
Passion: Committed in heart and mind
Diversity: As inclusive as our brands
Quality: What we do, we do well

Key Activities

After crafting the grand strategy, entrepreneurs should have a clear picture of the important activities of the business. To understand or define key activities, they may refer to Porter's value chain analysis. It is one of the most comprehensive frameworks that can design necessary activities for a company. For a startup, try to keep the main activities as lean as possible, the operation unit may need to handle all the important tasks as one cohesive unit. A startup should focus on primary activities to develop the core competency. At an early stage with limited resources, the founder may outsource certain secondary activities to 3rd party vendors, as the business expanding over time forms more specialized departments to serve the needs of larger business volume.

Primary Activities

Primary activities are the main activities that create goods or services. It comprises:

Inbound logistics–These are the tasks related to receiving, storing, and distributing inputs within the company. Fast and frequent delivery from the supplier helps to improve the inventory turnover. Relationships with the supplier are the key factor in creating value here.

Operations– These are the intermediary units that convert the inputs (raw material, half-finished goods) into products that customers purchase. The efficient operation unit shortens the time customers receive their products.

Outbound logistics–The activities that deliver your products to the customer. These are things like the collection, storage, and distribution systems by company logistics, and they may be internal within the company or external to your customer.

Marketing and sales–These are the processes you used to convince clients to purchase from you. The quality you offer, and how well you deliver the value proposition to them, differentiate your business from the competitors.

Service–These are the after-sales activities related to maintaining the value of output to customers.

Support Activities
These are the business support units established to support the primary functions in a company.
Procurement (purchasing)– It is the support unit gets the resources for business to operate. It includes finding the supplier and negotiating for the best prices.

Human-resource management- People are a significant asset to generate growth in business. It is important to attract and retain talent with good HR practices.

Technological development- Novel products and services developed in the process of research and development, to cope with the changing needs of the market. New technologies like machine learning, artificial intelligence and automation may change the way business produces goods or services.

Infrastructure- These are company support units that help to maintain business operation. It refers to a company management, finance, accounting, and even quality control unit.

Key resources

Physical resources are tangible assets that used to generate sales. Retailers with shop lots and goods display shelves are the superb examples. **Financial resources** are financial assets for funding like cash, loan, or raising bond and equity. **Intellectual properties** are the creation of the mind such as the brand name, logo, patent, invention. **Human resources** with different expertise and skill sets are the most important resources. Start-up has limited resources. Thus, it needs people with more broad skills to cope with multitasking environment. After identifying key activities, try to link relevant key resources to it. We will show a few examples of how to link key resources with key activity.

Product-driven business has products that serve a certain segment of customer. For instance, a pharmaceutical company may need to hire scientists to develop a drug. In its key activities, it may need to emphasize technological change to create the new patent drug.

Service/professional business delivering the value proposition based on its domain knowledge. For example, a software company needs programmers as its main employee. Their key activities must focus on developing a proprietary software program.

Key Activities	Key Resouces
Product Driven- Technological change Abbott- R&D for new patent drug	Human Resource: Scientists, Pharmarcist
	Intellectual property: Proprietary process, patent
	Physical resources: Laboratory & equipments
	Financial resources: Reseach grant,cash,loan,bond, equity.
Service- Technological change Amazon -Cloud service Technological change	Human Resource: IT specialist
	Intellectual property: Proprietary software, copyright, patent
	Physical resources: IT infrastucture, Server, Mainframe, PC
	Financial resources: cash,loan,bond, equity.
Infrastructure- logistics, procurement Walmart- Receive and distribution of stocks	Human Resource: Warehouse personnel, driver, cashier
	Intellectual property: Trademark, Brand logo
	Physical resources: Departmental store, Goods, Display shelf
	Financial resources: Cash,loan,bond, equity.

Key partners

Business needs key partners to optimize costs, achieve economies of scale, mitigate risks and gain strategic asset and activity to complement each other limited resources. Often times, a startup may not have the resources and expertise to produce goods on its own. It may need to outsource certain activity to the supplier or service provider.

For the supply of products, businesses cannot manufacture all goods on its own. It may need to find a supplier of the product at a lower cost to gain profit from the margin of difference. A good relationship with a supplier is important to get fast delivery, quality products and better credit term in payment.

For complex finished goods, even a large corporation may not have the resources to produce everything on their own. For instance, a personal computer manufacturer needs to get components from various vendors to assemble a PC. This is due to the supplier has a large demand for a product. Thus, it can achieve the scale of economies by saving fixed cost from its business units and able to offer the product at the competitive price.

If a business buys materials or components from a supplier, it also reduces the exposure of business risk to the unrelated business. It doesn't have to deal with price fluctuation of raw material in production. It also reduces unnecessary operation risk and other technical difficulties of the production process.

Chapter 3 - Value Proposition

Modern Elements of Value Propositions

We need to develop a unique value proposition to sell our products in today's competitive market. Generally, we may approach from how people perceive value.

Utility

Most people are rational in their spending. Most of us maximize utility in relation to quality of life and availability of money. That is, most of us will buy whatever we can afford to maintain our quality of life. The utility is perceived differently by the user's preference. The options that made by everyone's one of us might not be the same. It is considered rational if we can get what we like the most within our spending power. The utility can be measured in terms like productivity, price, prestige, durability, design, convenience, risk. The choices of utility must be optimized between the different criteria. For instance, premium products must have most high-end features; medium price products offer at least average or above-average features; low price products only offer basic utility features.

	Price		
Utility	High	Medium	Low
Productivity	High performance	Middle performance	Low performance
Prestige	Premium brand	Established brand	No Brand/ Not emphasize on Branding
Durability	Lost lasting, best material	Durable, quality material	Short live, inexpensive material
Design	Elegant, Estatic design	Decent design	Utility design
Convenience	Easy to use	Relatively easy to use	Need some effort to use
Risk	Low defective rate	Low defective rate	High defective rate

The New Economy

The value proposition must be established and delivered on a new form of technology. The Internet economy will continue to evolve substantially over the next decade, with the advent of new technology and business model. New disruptive technologies such as the Internet of Things (IoT), Artificial Intelligence (AI) and Blockchain will change the economy and job opportunity in the market. Entrepreneurs need to leverage these cutting-edge technologies to survive in the era of intense competition.

E-commerce

E-commerce is an Internet business, which involves the transfer of information on the trading of goods and services. The famous website such as BigCommerce, Wix, Volusion offer websites design service. They are among the best choices for designing an e-commerce website without an extensive programming language. They offer plans and built-in applications for customization of your business needs. Choose a plan and features that suit the business needs with minimal effort. Then, you can concentrate on marketing and sales of your website. The online marketplace such as Amazon, Alibaba, eBay, Lazada offers a ready platform with access to its large user base. Choose a category carefully so that your products serve the niche market well. These platforms normally charge a transaction fee and commission for the online sales. If you wish to avoid a lot of hassles for the inventory work, consider the drop ship model. It begins when you receive the order from the buyer and forward it to the trusted wholesaler. The wholesaler will do the delivery directly to your customer under your company name. At the end of the day, you gain the profit from arbitraging between the wholesale price and the retail selling price.

Sharing Economy

The main idea of sharing economic is that the limited resources can be used by different people when the need arises. It helps to prevent asset underutilization. With small one-time payment, people gain access without owning the resources. Sharing economy relies on digital technology to allocate resources efficiently according to the demand. It is the new means of doing business.

With the advent of mobile, PC applications and Internet network, sharing economy grew significantly. It becomes an integral part of our daily life. Uber, the ride-sharing business utilizing driver personal vehicles to fetch passenger. It helps the driver to earn more money during their spare time. Airbnb provides a platform for cozy homestay as an alternative lodging option to the traveler with a lower budget. At the same time, property owners earn extra income from the rent. Co-working spaces share working office for an entrepreneur with a minimum fee. Providers even offer other infrastructure, secretary service, courier and mailing service, etc. to start up founder. Peer to peer lending and crowdfunding provide alternative funding for individuals and business owners with lower credit requirements to get the necessary funding.

Co-creation is a unique form of sharing economy. It involves the participation of end users and relevant stakeholders, in the development process of the final output. From the identification of the problem to implementation of the solution, end-users play the main role create output according to their context. The co-creation process generally takes two important steps. Firstly, users submit their contribution to the company. Secondly, the company selects the most appealing ideas as their final output. At the end of the process, the company developed a more customer-centric output to the market. On the other hand, the end users gained either a one-time prize or even co-ownership rights of the final output. Thus, it is a win-win strategy for both parties in the long run.

Increasing competition from sharing economy firms has forced many incumbents to revamp current business models and finding innovative ways to bring value to their customers. The value proposition can be delivered via the sharing economy benefiting the owner of the resource, platform provider and its consumer.

Experience Economy

Experiences often come with services, but experiences are a distinct form of economic offering, as services are mostly related to the offering of goods together with it. An experience happens when a company utilizes the service as the platform, and goods as tools, to engage consumers in a pleasant and unforgettable event. Experiences are unique. Consumers gain different experiences as the results of the interaction between their inner-mind and the event. The value propositions are delivered in a unique way to the consumers. Consumption of music industry evolves rapidly from the album records to digital format.

As the singer gains popularity, the concert can be held as staging experience to audiences. Nowadays, most lucrative incomes for most famous singers are revenues from the mega concert. Tickets charge at premium price generated more revenues than conventional record sales. Experience economy selling a service more than its basic form. Consumers perceive the unique experiences as an offer more than its monetary worth. Most singers staging their talent as a variety show more than just singing in a concert. So, the consumers often willing to pay more to engage in real-life experience more than any virtual word interaction.

Freemium Economy

Freemium business model is common in-service industry where free users enjoy the basic features of the offering. Only the premium users pay the nominal fee to enjoy the additional features of the service. For instance, Linkedin is a free professional social service platform, the company targeting different category of consumers such as job applicants, employers, advertisers, and headhunters to entice them to pay for the service.

Another form of the freemium company doesn't really charge the users; they charge the advertisers in the business model. Ordinary Facebook users enjoy the social media platform for free, while the businesses pay the advertisement fee to Facebook. Google is another good example of a freemium company. Users search online content with no cost, but the businesses pay the advertisement fee to appear on the top search list.

Freemium company generally requires a large base of consumers to promote their offering. For the survival of the company, they must maintain a certain level of conversion rate to cover the marginal cost per user. Thus, entrepreneurs need to create the value proposition optimizing the features for free and paid user according to their budget.

Influencer Economy

Influencer economy is a form of marketing using the credibility of influential people to attract consumers. They can reach many consumers via direct or indirect interaction on online or offline media as their "idol." As these people have influence over potential customers' opinion and their purchase decision based on trust.

Influencer economy depends on how many followers whom an influencer connects with. The impact on purchase decision is stronger when the influencer making more frequent contact with their follower. The credibility and expertise are higher when the influencer is the subject matter expert, which in turn translated into sales. The persuasiveness of the influencer also plays a big role in consumer buying intention.

Branding using Corporate Social Responsibility (CSR)

CSR initiatives build customer loyalty based on high moral and ethical values. Some companies use CSR as a strategic tool to gain customer support for their presence in global markets, helping them achieve the competitive advantage by using social contributions as a form of publicity.

CSR activities can be implemented via charities' activity like sponsoring causes and disadvantaged groups such as disabled people; women; children; refugees; minorities; indigenous peoples; migrant workers; elderly groups, etc. CSR initiatives can also practice via an environmentally friendly approach. It helps to reduce waste and pollution of our planet. "Green" manufacturing emphasizes utilizing renewable energy to reduce the carbon footprint; reusing and recycling to reduce waste, minimizing natural resource and pollution to the environment.

Instead of prioritizing profit, CSR initiatives emphasize people, planet, and profit. It is a comprehensive approach to achieve competitiveness and sustainable growth at the same time. The company emphasizes on CSR initiatives create unique value propositions that enticing conscious consumers in modern society.

Scarcity

People value a resource as precious when they find it difficult to get access to it. The law of supply and demand explains the interaction between the supply and the demand for a resource. Generally, low supply and high demand raise the price. On the contrary, ample supply and poor demand cause the price to fall. For instance, airfare during peak season is more expensive than off peak-season. We may focus on how to create this phenomenon changing the customer's perception of value.

For products, entrepreneurs may sell the products far away from the source of its origin. A higher price can be charged at the inland city-center seafood restaurant than a coastal restaurant. The retailer charges a premium price on imported products or sells to overseas market.

Limited time offer creates a sense of scarcity. It creates a sense of urgency of the customer to purchase within the promotion period. Limited resources also trigger the purchase intention. Low quantity indicates the item is fast moving. People will be tempted to do the purchase before the item sold out. The pre-release marketing campaign is another way to create a sense of scarcity. Smartphone manufacturer such as Apple using the pre-order sales to generate hype before the actual release of the products. This strategy also enables the producer to estimate the demand for the new phone.

Mass customization of products/services based on customer preference also another form of scarcity marketing. When the outputs are exclusive to the customer, it creates what the customer really wants. Customers often willing to pay more since it changes the perception of value on their mind with the exclusive product. It might have great influence on emotional attachment, which in turn affected loyalty on the products/services.

Cultural elements

Language can be either spoken or written. One of the most crucial developments in the civilized society was the creation of written language. If you wish to introduce the product to a foreign country, you may need to find a translator to do the translation for the marketing materials. It is important that the value proposition can be delivered as intended in the context of the foreign language.

Cultural norms are the standards and expectations for behaving in society. Formal norms are the most important standard of behavior in any society as governed by the rule of law. In most countries, it includes criminal law, civil law, traffic laws. Informal norms refer as standards of behavior that are less important such as the folkway and custom. Mannerisms are everyday behaviors as how we interact with people. It is one example of informal norms. A good business value proposition must not go against any social norms of society.

Different cultures have rituals, or established procedures, ceremonies and festive seasons according to their own calendar. Value propositions deliver via cultural elements create more business opportunities in the diverse ethnic group in the market.

The framework of Value Proposition

The framework of the value proposition is summarized in a concise table, using the consumer's buying experience (i.e. from purchase until disposal), and modern elements of value proposition that we discussed before. It helps entrepreneurs identify important elements to create a compelling value proposition. This framework also creates a unique selling proposition to consumers.

Value Proposition Design Products/Services	Utility	New Economy Model	Cultural Elements	CSR initiatives	Scarcity
Purchase	Price: High/Medium/Low	E-commerce- online store Sharing Economy- using online apps to allocate resources	Different language marketing material Festive offer	Contribution to charity and vulnerable group	Pre order- create sense of anticipation Limited offer- create the sense of urgency to buy
Using the product/service	Productivity- increase the productive effort and performance Prestige- Pride to user Durability-Withstand pressure, damage, wear and tear Design- Savvy and elegant Convenience- easy to use, hassle free Low risk- harmless to user	Sharing Economy- prevent underutilization of resources Influencer economy- entice user using influential people Experience economy- create unique user experience Freemium model- free basic features for most user Co-Creation model- create new product/service from user's idea	Different language product/service Not against any law & social norm	Environmental friendly Low carbon Foot print, zero emission No harm to user physically or mentally	Mass Customization- create unique product/service for customer
After sales service	Exchange and refund policy Warranty(on site/ off site) Complaint and feedback	Co-Creation model- improve product from customer feedback	Different language support	Reliability and quality of product and service	Individual solution for customer
Disposal	Easy to dispose No Extra Cost	Sharing economy- sharing the unwanted items for recycling, or others in need	Cultural access and attitude toward recyling and waste management	Recylable & Reusable material	Special disposal service for customer

Chapter 4 -Customer

Customer Segmentation

Generally, there are two approaches to marketing. In the undifferentiated strategy, all customers are targeted using one marketing strategy, without any specific efforts to serve any groups. A single marketing mix is implemented using the same price, product, placement, and similar promotional effort - to gain most of the consumers in the mass market. This may work only when the product/service is universal with the standard feature.

In today's competitive market, entrepreneurs often need to focus on several customer segments with differentiated strategy. From the segmentation, entrepreneurs can determine the profit of each section of customer by analyzing its revenues and costs. With the information, the necessary resources can be allocated to marketing activity, to match the needs of different customer segments. The segment performances must be evaluated so that the new plan can be made according to the market conditions over time. The appropriate customer segmentations allow the entrepreneurs to understand on how to satisfy the needs of customers, predict their future purchase decision, allocate the required resources, identify opportunities to optimize the marketing campaign, monitor growth patterns of important customers and track sales performance over time.

Proper customer segmentation helps entrepreneurs to build distribution channels, design products or services features, determine pricing strategy to suit the needs of a different segment of consumers. Thus, customer segmentation is important to subdivide the market into meaningful segments, according to their geographic, demographic, psychographic and behavioral profiles.

Geographic segmentation

Geographic segmentation segregates markets according to geographical features. Entrepreneurs can divide markets from as vast as continents to be as small as postcode or even street address. Geographic segmentation is common in international marketing where marketers decide their offering according to countries. Geographical segmentation subdivided to state, city, town, population density, and climatic zone. By combining demographic and geographic segmentation, geo-demographic segregation may derive more insights from a different group of consumers.

Demographic segmentation

Demographic segregation divides consumers according to the structure of the population. The demographic profiles such as age, gender, income, occupation, race, marital status, family size, etc. are among the common structure of a population. Consumers with the same profile often exhibit similar purchasing habit that translating into preferences on products or services. Practically, demographic segmentation can be done using those variables available on the national census study.

Psychographic segmentation

Psychographics is a combination of psychology and demographics of consumers. Psychographic information is the psychology of consumers who derive from the structure of the population. Demographics explain the dry facts from the structure of the population, while psychographics describes the purchase behavior that derives from the demographics of consumers. Entrepreneurs can only reach the target consumers when they understand both demographics and psychology of the consumers. It is necessary applying the rule of association to link both types of data.

Lifestyle elements like activities, interests, and opinions also affect consumers purchase decision. Different consumers might have distinct preferences on **activities and interests** based on their education level. If the more educated consumers like reading, they might choose diverse genres based on their own interest and professional background. Thus, activities, interests, and opinions inform us a lot about a consumer's purchase decision.

Consumers can be categorized into different social classes. This depends mainly on their purchasing power. It is also affected by the occupation, income as well as their spending habits. Consumers always buy what they can afford to maintain their social class. Therefore, premium brands target wealthy consumers because only these people would be the classes capable of buying their products. It often needs to emphasize lifestyle, social class, and branding.

Behavioral Segmentation

Behavioral segmentation segregates the consumers based on patterns of behavior displayed as they purchase from a company. It allows businesses to divide consumers into the categories according to the attitude, response when consuming a product or service. Common behavioral variables include purchase history such as purchase frequency based on the number of purchases in a certain period.

User status is another option to classify customers by their relationship with the business. It can be subdivided into festive consumers, non-festive consumers based on purchase records. The behavior classification on users' status can also be members, non-members, one-time users, regular users depend on their interaction with the business.

Through behavioral data, customers can be subdivided by loyalty based on purchase history. Loyal customers are the biggest sales contributors & brand advocates. They are the perfect target group for loyalty programs that offer special privileges, rewards, and discount, to strengthen the customer relationship and incentivize continued future business. Thus, from an economic point of view, it is relatively cheaper to retain them than acquire a new customer.

Interest-based behavioral segmentation is important to deliver personalized experiences that keep customers coming back for more purchases. It is applicable whether your aim is to increase product consumption, cross-sell or up-sell to your consumers, or deliver the marketing content and facilitate them to purchase more. One of the greatest advantages of interest behavior is the ability to connect specific interests with the intent of purchase.

Machine learning can help to scale up the process. As an increasing number of consumers engage and interact, there will be more interest-based data capture and learn over time to produce more accurate suggestion in the recommender system. Netflix, Amazon, and Google use recommendation system for suggesting content and products based on customers' interests. Each time you collect customers' data, you may associate with the number of additional potential interests, that might be effective for engaging the customer with related products using the collaborative filtering approach. Using the behavioral segmentation methods described above, you can make marketing campaigns more efficient, maximize ROI, increase customer lifetime value and build a deeper knowledge to retain your customer.

Customer Relationship

Customer relationship management (CRM) is an approach to manage the entire customer relationship, including the purchase process, post-sales service, feedback and recommendations to all customers. It aims to improve business relationships with customers, particularly focusing on **customer retention** and ultimately driving sales growth. CRM must be pragmatic in terms of scale and budget. Launching highly focused projects with narrow scopes and modest goals is a more practical approach. Entrepreneurs must be investing heavily in solving clearly defined problems within the customer relationship cycle—the activities that run from the segmenting and targeting of customers all the way through to retain them.

In a larger firm, customer relationships are handled by the customer service department in the form of employee-customer interaction. Personal assistance is assigned during sales and/or after sales for a company with bigger budget to foster a better relationship with the customer. For a start-up, an entrepreneur can offer dedicated private assistance to the customer. It is the most intimate and hands-on personal assistance in which the entrepreneur or sales personnel is assigned to handle all the inquiries and needs of clients. It requires more effort and time, but it helps to nurture the relationship with customers and retain them over time.

Create a community facilitating the interactions among the customers and company. The community platform sharing knowledge and solving problems between customers via **social listening**. It requires regular and consistent efforts such as monitoring conversations, analyzing feedbacks, answering questions and solving issues. Co-creation is viable in an active community where the member input is incorporated into the final output of the company. The community members can research the products/services, engage with others to solve issues and post comments on the output. These communities are the best way to create customer-centric output. It is also a method to empower the customers to serve themselves and make them feel connected with the communities and loyal to your brand.

Chapter 5 Channels

A company can deliver its value proposition to different segments of customers via its own or partner channel. Productive channels will generate a company's sales in ways that are quick, inexpensive and efficient. Channel management is a method of trading, delivering your products using various marketing and sales technique to reach possible customers. A business must determine the goal of each channel and define the specific framework for each of the channels to produce the desired results. Identifying the customer segment linked to each channel also helps to determine the best products/ services to pitch to those channels.

Channel Strategy

A channel strategy is the action plan for reaching customers with products and services. The design of the channel plan must consider factors such as customer preference; competitor in the market; constraints such as costs, resources, and capabilities. Proper channel strategy aims to develop a relationship with customers to gain repeat sales and increases the profitability of an existing customer. The successful channel strategy often streamlines communication between the business and customer. To achieve this, the segmentation is important for selection of the target group. After the selection, the right marketing mix with the customized channel can be delivered to serve the customer better. The objective of channel management is to establish direct communication with customers in each channel. If the company achieves this goal, it creates the best marketing channels that suit with diverse customer segment. The techniques utilized in every channel could be different, but the overall strategy must deliver the value proposition of business consistently.

Direct Channel

Brick and click model

Entrepreneurs who are product manufacturers or service providers have a few channel options. The easiest way is the direct channel in which they sell to the customer without any intermediary channels. Opening physical store by locating near customers is one of the choices. For example, a pharmaceutical company that sells medicinal products can locate sales offices near major hospitals and clinics. The suppliers may also employ a sales force to close deals with customers or sell its products or services through e-commerce websites, mobile applications. Direct selling via door to door represents another option, although this business model has been replaced by e-commerce. Combining your online and offline business such that they complement with each other as bricks and clicks model. For instance, physical stores may be used for delivery and after-sales service for web orders. On the other hands, the e-commerce store can be used by the retail store to extend inventory, product range and expand customer base beyond the geographical reach.

Dropship model

Recently, a new type of online retailer known as "drop shipper" has become very popular, especially to the individual seller. Drop shipper is a retailer who doesn't keep any stock but generates online sales and earns commission from the wholesale supplier. The biggest advantage of this retail fulfillment method is that the entrepreneur doesn't have to bear the expenses on inventory and other related overhead costs of a traditional retailer. Drop shipper simply passes the order to the wholesale partner who handles the product delivery and takes a commission from the sales. eCommerce business that runs on a drop shipping model is largely dependent on wholesale suppliers and needs to be careful about sourcing the credible partner.

Omnichannel

Omnichannel is a cross-channel integration business model that companies deploy to improve the overall customer experience. Rather than working in isolation, all channels and the supporting units are designed to cooperate with each other. To deploy omnichannel, the action plan does not need to incorporate all available channels, which is impractical. Instead, it involves the integration of all channels using available resources and capabilities such that the customer experience across multiple channels is pleasant and efficient than using single channel independently.

It is important to incorporate the multiple channels as one cohesive strategy that creates the integrated customer experience. For instance, the customer can be shopping in a physical store, the online store from a desktop or mobile device, or by social media, or by telephone, and the experience would be seamless from any channels.

Omnichannel has wide applications across various industries such as healthcare, financial services, government agency, telecom, and retail industries. Companies that utilize omnichannel often need to create a unique selling proposition that engages with customers via multiple avenues simultaneously.

Indirect channels-Distribution Partners Value-added sellers

Entrepreneurs can also generate sales via indirect channels involving one or more intermediaries. They can sell via value-added seller (VARs). VARs are companies that bundle different products and services and resale them as a turn-key solution to end users. It is referred to as one tier distribution system since it involves only one level of the middleman. In the two-tier distribution system, the entrepreneur sells to wholesaler/distributor, which, in turn sells to VARs and finally to the end user.

The value can be created by customizing, integrating, consulting, training and implementation of professional services. The value can also be added by customizing the application for the product designed for the customer's preference which is then resold as a new package. For instance, VARs develop platform software to incorporate other vendors' software packages.

The term turnkey is often used in the IT industry, where a company purchases all the necessary components and builds a fully operational system for end users. By doing this, the company has added value above the cost of the individual components and sells it at the premium price to end users.

Customers would purchase the system from the reseller if they don't have time and skill to assemble the entire system themselves.

Wholesaler

The wholesaler is a middleman that buys in large quantities from a supplier or producer and resells at a wholesale price to a retailer. An entrepreneur with excess production capacity may choose to sell in bulk quantity to the wholesaler. Wholesalers normally specialize in a certain type of product or sell a broad range of stocks to retailers in different industries. A wholesaler that only stock non-competing products for a brand are known as sole distributors. Besides breaking bulk quantities orders into a smaller package, wholesalers can also assemble or package goods as part of the value-added process to the retailer. Wholesalers typically store products in a warehouse for shorter periods of time compared to distributors.

Licensing

Licensing enables an entrepreneur to access the broader customer base instantly by leveraging existing production, distribution, and marketing systems that other companies build over time. Licensing fees typically amount to only a small percentage of royalty, but it can add up substantially when the volume of sales is large. The intellectual property owner (licensor) must ensure that the partner (licensee) has the resources, capabilities, and commitment to deliver the product or service with the same capacity as the owner. Intellectual property licensing is common in the industry such as broadcasting, publication, software, academia and high-tech industry involving technology transfer.

A licensor also may grant permission to a licensee to use the trademark or brand without the fear of infringement claim from the licensor. With the license, the licensee can use the trademark to gain the established market share. The license often depends on specific contractual terms such as a geographic region, a period of time or certain scope of business.

Franchising

Franchising is a special form of licensing, which can be divided into two main categories. In a product distribution model, the franchisor sells finished products to the franchisee and permits them to use their brand and trademark. In return, the franchisees buy a minimum order of quantity of products or pay fees to the franchisor. Most of the time, the franchisee does not receive the full support to run the business and require developing sales service independently in this model. The product franchise model is quite similar to a supplier-dealer relationship, with a few differences in the relationship. The franchisee may sell products on an exclusive or semi-exclusive basis and receive support from the franchisor. The automobile industry is a typical example of the product distribution franchise.

In business format franchises, the franchisee utilizes franchisor's brand name and trademark. Furthermore, the franchisee gains the complete system of the franchisor including operations, marketing, inventory, support, etc. This model is the more consistent way of achieving sustainable results for the franchisee. The franchisee is often empowered with a detailed plan that entails the entire operation of the franchise. Besides, the franchisee is provided with training and support on advertising, marketing, management of the premises, recruitment, training of staff, and even standard operating procedure of the franchise.

Original equipment manufacturers (OEMs), managed service providers (MSPs), consultants, systems integrators (SIs), independent software vendor(ISVs) may also serve as indirect channel partners. Entrepreneur pursuing these alternative channels will often need to create a partner program to manage relationships to avoid conflict of interest.

Original equipment manufacturers (OEM)

Original Equipment Manufacturer (OEM) is a company that produces parts or equipment that may be sold under another manufacturer brand name. Entrepreneurs with excess manufacturing capacity may choose to be OEM by distributing their products more to other companies.

OEM is common in software distribution. For example, Microsoft sells the retail version of Windows operating system (OS) to end users via their platform. On the other hand, the OEM version of Windows OS often bundled with a personal computer (PC) in the market. Warranty terms might be different for retail and OEM version.

OEM drives down the unit cost of the product by manufacturing bulk quantities to achieve the scale of economies. On the other hand, using OEM products allow the partner company to get the needed products or components without owning and operating a highly complex business activity.

Managed service provider (MSP)

A managed service provider (MSP) is a company that manages a client's IT infrastructure or systems, regularly and under a subscription model. MSP often charges for the services under different packages such as per-device, per-user, number of features, projects or all-inclusive pricing. Entrepreneurs may choose to outsource certain business processes that require high cost & expertise to MSP, to expand the existing channel.

Systems integrators (SI)

A system integrator (SI) is a person or company that specializes in integrating components such as hardware, software, networking and so that those subsystems function as an integrated system. Using system integrator, a company can obtain cheaper, pre-configured components and different software as one unified solution to fulfill the business objectives, in contrast to more expensive, customized application that may require unique components or programming skills.

An integrated solution can also simplify the complex process of sourcing and dealing with multiple vendors. Otherwise, the standalone systems needed to purchase and manage independently. Hence, systems integration reduces the tedious process of both procurement and technical issues. Entrepreneurs may often need SI assistance to do integration across the system of multiple channels.

Independent software vendor (ISV)

Generally, the independent software vendors are often the companies that developing software with specialized niche offerings. For Instance, they can focus on making the specific business unit applications (HR, Accounting, IT, Marketing, procurement), or industry software (manufacturer, wholesaler, retailer) software for either goods or service providers. There is also ISV providing a highly customized solution, such as data migration utilities, networking, point of sales system, etc.

An independent software vendor program will generally offer a mix of technical and specialized domain knowledge application for a software platform such as Microsoft, Linux, Google, etc. ISV software may include in areas such as technology training, briefings on product development roadmaps, specific pricing and licensing terms, product discounts and co-marketing initiatives. A platform provider also offers ISV approval seal via software validation programs.

Generally, an independent software vendor program operates within a platform vendor's business partner program. Such programs aim to cover a spectrum of partner relationships and interactions to leverage joint strengths, convert them into incremental business opportunities of the platform software. While ISVs customize specialized software that is added to its platform's software, original equipment manufacturers use platform components to build products for another manufacturer under their brand name. Value-added resellers incorporate platform software into their own software product packages. And managed service providers remotely monitor and install hardware and software platforms at the end customer's location, and may also provide software as a service on the cloud platform.

Indirect channels-Distribution Marketing Partners
Affinity Marketing Partnership

This can be a modified form of distribution marketing partnership by introducing unique offers to the target group of consumers. These offers typically contain a package of products or services that align with the consumers' purchasing preferences.

An easy example of this is when a cinema and a credit card company working together. The credit card company is looking forward to establishing a new customer base: particularly, cinema customer who never had a credit card before. So, they partner with a cinema operator to offer their specialized product, such as a credit card developed especially for cinema customer. The card would most likely be branded with the cinema's logo, and special incentives are offered to cinema customer when they use their credit card to pay for a movie ticket, food, and beverage at the cinema.

Affinity marketing partnerships allow the partner brands collaborating to offer unique discounts, services and/or products to target customers related to the partners' brands, as such they will have a high probability for purchasing the products.

Sponsorship Marketing Partnership

In a sponsorship marketing partnership, one partner advertises its brand on the other entity typically the media company, big sport event, charity events for publicity. For example, electrical company Hisense is the sponsor for FIFA world cup 2018.

Affiliate Marketing Partnership

The company with e-commerce business can reach more customers via the affiliate program. They may use their partner's network to tap into different customer segments. In most cases, affiliate marketing partners can help to expand sales beyond the geographical regions or customer segments.

A partner who offers affiliate programs often gets commission or referral fee from its e-commerce partner on products sold and leads generated. To compensate for the commission cost, some companies choose to raise their offering price, while others maintain their price by absorbing the cost themselves. Most of the marketing and advertising companies offer affiliate programs; among the popular ones are Commission Junction, LinkShare, Rakuten.

Partner Relationship Management

Channel conflicts often arise between channels that are perceived as counterproductive or unfair. For example, e-commerce business partner who undercuts the retail partners' profit. To reduce the pricing advantage of e-commerce channel, the vendor must allow a retail partner to have new items weeks before they are available on the e-commerce platform to compensate for the traditional retailer higher overhead expenses. Other than that, the vendor may also provide the training to build an e-commerce platform for a retailer to increase the sales via click and mortar approach.

Channel conflict comes in many forms. For the less severe case, it is merely the necessary moves to maintain the competitiveness of the business environment. It is positive for the manufacturer to remain relevant in the market via forcing obsolete or uneconomic dealers to adapt or decline. Other severe conflicts, however, can be detrimental to the manufacturer's business model. These high-risk conflicts generally happen when there are overlapping customer segments already served by an existing channel causing the cannibalization of product. This causes the decline of channel economics that the threatened channel partner either stops selling the product or even selling the product of a competitor. An entrepreneur who crafting the channel strategy must strike a balance of both direct and indirect channels to avoid potential channel conflict.

Chapter 6- Revenues

Revenues

Revenue is the income generated from sale activity of goods and services. It often involves the transfer of ownership or access rights from seller to user when the payment is made for the products or services. Revenue is typically shown as the top item (top line) in the profit and loss statement from which all other expenses are deducted to get net income (bottom line).

Generally, there are seven main ways of creating revenue: asset sales, usage fees, subscription fees, lending/leasing/renting, licensing, brokerage fees, and advertising. The entrepreneur may choose the appropriate revenue stream according to the business nature through the application of the value proposition framework (See Chapter 3).

Asset sale

An asset sale is completed, when the buyer obtains the goods delivered by a company. Asset Sale – the most common type involves the sale of a current asset which is a part of the inventory. Selling ownership rights of tangible goods to consumers is quite normal for a retailer. For example, an asset sale occurs when a computer store delivers a Personal Computer to a customer. By doing this, the customer owns a PC for personal use.

It is difficult to differentiate between companies according to whether they sell services or goods in the today competitive market. A more useful way to make the distinction is focusing on the *intangibles* and *tangibles*. Entrepreneur sells intangibles to consumers, no matter what is manufactured in the factory. While some of the dissimilarity might seem apparent, it is obvious that there are a lot of similarities between the marketing of intangibles and tangibles.

The key area of similarity in the marketing of intangibles and tangibles revolves around the intangibility. Marketing is often associated with getting new customers and keeping the existing customers. The degree of product intangibility has its greatest effect in both areas.

The intangibility of all products

The intangibles can determine the product's success, even with mature consumer goods like shampoo, and frozen food. If it is not functioned as intended, for instance, a shampoo is not cleaned as advertised, or frozen food cannot be eaten as stated in the label, the results can be terrible. User can't experience in advance the moderate-to-low-priced goods such as canned foods or detergents. To convince buyers more comfortable with the tangibles that can't be tested, companies must go beyond the actual promises of specifications, using advertisements, and labels to provide reassurance of the products' utility.

Packaging is one common tool to visualize the intangibility. For Instance, honey put into see-through glass jars, cookies into sealed-windowed boxes, canned goods get a strong appetizing photo and label on the surface of the packaging. In all cases, the main idea is to provide a reassuring effect on tangibility for what's promised but can't be directly delivered before the sale.

Common sense shows us, and the academic study indicates that people use the appearances to make judgments of their real world. It does not matter whether the product is expensive or cheap, whether the product is complex or easy to use, whether the buyers are tech savvy or ignorant, or whether they buy for themselves or others. Everybody relies on both physical appearances and impressions to make a purchase decision.

The product will be gauged in two major parts—not by just which the company is but also the people who represent it. The company and its people are both parts of the "product" that customers must consider before they buy. The less tangible the product, the more powerfully and persistently the judgment about it gets shaped by the packaging—how it's displayed, who presents it, and what's implied by metaphor, symbol, and other replacement for the tangibility of the product.

The way the product is presented in the sales process (how it is shown in the brochure, letter, design appearance), how it is presented by people, and by whom—all these become critical components of the product and influence the customer purchase intention.

Service Revenue

Service Revenue refers to income earned from providing intangible products or services such as technical services, consulting or other specialist services as a part of the trade, profession or business. It is the main source of income for service-oriented businesses. It could take the form of monthly bills or even a commercial contract. For example, a monthly mobile phone contract, unless the contract is terminated or the customers do not pay on time, the service providers can gain the recurring sales for the agreed period.

You may offer a service at a low introductory price or even freemium to grow your customer base and as lead generation tool for the other more expensive services. Lastly, provide a service that leverage on your experiences, skillsets, and the things that you are good at. You may need to figure out what you're good at and find an appealing way to sell it repeatedly.

Subscription

Subscription-A company sells the repeated access to a product or a service. For Instance, Telco companies generally sell a phone bundled with data and talk plan through a monthly subscription. Subscription business model was pioneered by traditional media such as magazines and newspapers. This model is enticing because a contract binds the user to pay consistently for the product or service. It means that a company can make much more recurring revenue.

The entrepreneurs may sell one-off basis or periodic access of services to the customer. For instance, a theatre sells the subscription pass as the package deal to the customer. A one-time sale of the pass turns into a recurring sale that builds brand loyalty. The user is tracked in both a subscribed and unsubscribed status within the business to grow member base over time.

Membership of a certain type of organizations or any other special interest groups are also known as subscriptions. For instance book clubs, music clubs, cable television, satellite television, satellite radio, mobile network operators, internet providers, software, websites (e.g., blogging websites), business solutions providers, financial services firms, health clubs, as well as the media such as newspapers, magazines, and academic journals. Renewal of a subscription may be activated by period selectively or activated automatically, the payment can be settled by a pre-authorized credit card or via bank account.

For a web-based application, the freemium model is common by providing the basic features for free access, but restrict access of premium features to the free users. It can be applied to both unlimited and periodic access. For unrestricted access, an entrepreneur must ensure the availability and consistency of the subscribed features. For periodic access, the web-based application must be updated from in terms of contents, features and providing continuous support for user consistently to retain them. At the same time, it helps to generate recurring revenues for the company.

In terms of circulation of the subscription, an entrepreneur can control the circulation of the subscription to increase the revenue by a number of devices for a subscription. For instance, Microsoft office 365 basic plan is now limited to 365 days for five devices. For unlimited access,

Microsoft office software limits one license for each device.

Lending

The private lending business model is more viable when you focus locally. Most of your loans should come from within the city or even from the local community. Determine the funding capacity of your investor. If it is between $1 000 to $100 000, then set this as the niche market. Other than that, if your clients need the fund of $1000, provide the same amount loan with an attractive interest rate with fast approval, minimum paperwork for them to get the money instantly.

Build business gradually with a small loan, creating more volume than offering a larger loan. You can create more earnings by doing the transactions of the microloan. As the big loan client often has higher bargaining power and requires a lower interest rate, causing the drop interest earnings. If you focus on more transactions with clients with good payback records, you actually diversifying the risk and minimize the probability of default loan.

Be specific in advertising and marketing with the local community of the type of loan and the loan amounts. Build the trustworthiness of your business within the community, design a website with photos and testimonials on actual deals your company has funded. Show the testimonials with your names, addresses, pictures, and email addresses for all clients to see it on the website. Use the phone number and postcode to show your locality attracting nearby clients. Attend industry seminars and seek advice from those who have succeeded in the business. Hire an industry expert to review your business practices and legal compliance with state and federal regulations. Conduct this business with integrity, and soon you will have a steady base of customers with the reputation build within the community.

Renting

Renting has long been a well-known moneymaking business because most people can't afford to purchase a high-value asset. However, they can afford to spend a small amount of money to gain access. Typical rental businesses include tools, watercraft, construction equipment, recreational vehicles, lodgings, musical instruments, office furniture and equipment, canoes and kayaks, camping equipment.

Start-up costs can be substantial depending on the asset you purchase to rent. However, you can reduce costs by purchasing used assets in good condition. Alternatively, you may even gather the owners of the assets to establish a rental pool, keeping a portion of the management fees for providing the services. Avoid idle inventory at all costs–it only occupies storage space and cash flow you could use to grow your business! Don't overspend on equipment initially: buy your minimum viable inventory based on your market research. Instead of buying the asset with cash, purchase it using the available financing scheme. Once your business gets bigger, buy the equipment that is more popular, lucrative based on customer preference. It is cheaper and easier to buy more equipment later than to get rid of excess and obsolete asset/equipment.

    Starting the similar business in two locations can lead to distinct business requirements. A car rental in the city will have different customers than one in the suburban area. So, make sure you know the target customers' need. Other than that, you may offer extra service related to your business. Contact the related businesses for referral partnership. Find partners with quality products and services to ensure the customer satisfaction for recurring sales. For instance, car rental customers might need the service of the eatery, data roaming, accommodation, a ticket to a tourist spot, activities of interest, etc. By referring customers to each other business. You create a win-win situation that both parties get more customers. Your customers get the one-stop solution and easy access to services and products they need.

So, while you want to make sure you have good insurance coverage for the rental assets. The customers are your largest risk too. Even with no-liability waivers, make sure you cover the rental services with the right insurance to protect the customer. In the event of unforeseen circumstances, the insurance claims may provide necessary compensation without using a large sum of your company's cash.

For the asset maintenance, you may need to schedule regular preventive maintenance. It is important for the quality and safety of the rental service. In case of the sudden breakdown, fix any issues promptly and completely with your own maintenance team or outsourced professionals to prevent the future breakdown. Cosmetic maintenance is important for the appeal of your rental asset, make sure your assets look like new to create a nice impression to potential customers.

    Rental agreements are an important document to clarify the terms and conditions like the specification of the asset, duration, fee, security deposits, insurance indemnification, and penalty term. You need to communicate terms and conditions to the customer before handling over the asset to them. Customers often need to sign the hard copy or website agreement. It is an important document to protect the mutual interest of both parties.

Make sure you create a good impression to potential customers. Rentals are recurring business–most customers only use the asset for a short period, so if they need to use the asset later, they have to rent again. Make sure that when they need the service, they become your repeat customers! Create a unique proposition to make your customers feel welcome and give them one-stop solution service with friendly customer support. Create a hassle-free experience–don't frustrate your customers with tons of paperwork and procedures. If you've followed all of this advice, you already have a nice overall idea by now, about what you should do to create a successful rental business.

Leasing

Leasing business model typically involves three main parties, i.e. the seller, the buyer and financier /bank. The seller contracts with the buyer of the periodic fees during the tenure. At the end of the payment, the seller may reclaim the ownership or transfer it to the buyer. Leasing business is common in transactions involving the exchange of expensive assets such as the medical device and industrial equipment. There are the two main markets for the leasing of equipment. "Big-ticket items" such as heavy machinery, commercial vehicles, diagnostic equipment and devices, manufacturing equipment, and physical infrastructure like commercial property, solar power systems are typical examples of items that may generate income through leasing arrangements.

    Because of the long leasing period, leasing arrangements require the collaborative relationships between sellers and lessors. Quality control is important in leasing arrangements since it requires the asset to perform consistently. Often a service agreement drafted requiring the seller to provide technical support and service maintenance throughout the term of the contract. Because contracts extend over a long duration, recurring sales from the same customer is an important source of income. Thus, sellers of leased equipment rely heavily on relationship-building with customer service and after-sales-service to gain trust from customers. Operating with leasing revenue requires sales personnel to focus on generating repeat sales in the form of lease renewals or extended period of leasing arrangements. The cost of financing is another important success factor, leasing business requires the participation of a financial institution for funding since it is capital intensive.

  Leasing agreement is often complex. All stakeholders need to understand the contract to prevent confusion and dispute. Leasing is a great business model for expanding the market for expensive items to customers who lack a large sum of cash or prefer financing. Besides that, leasing is a viable business model in most high-value items, since it absorbs the high processing cost and operational expenses gradually via financing.

Broker

The entrepreneur may generate income via intermediation service as the broker via an online or offline service. Brokers are market-makers: They facilitate transactions between buyers and sellers. Brokers play a major role in consumer-to-consumer (C2C), business-to-business (B2B), business-to-consumer (B2C) business. Typically, brokers charge a nominal fee or commission for each transaction fulfill in the market. They can charge the commission at a different rate from one industry to another. Brokerage fees are income created from an intermediary service via the order fulfillment between buyer and seller. For example, a property agent gains commission based on a percentage of property value.

Marketplace brokers are agents who provide a full range of services. Their service ranges from advisory service, market assessment to negotiation and fulfillment, for a particular industry. The marketplace can operate by a company, or an industry consortium with the big players in the industry. For example, an insurance agent works for a particular insurance company; an insurance broker may work for different insurance companies.

Demand collection system is the business model pioneered by Priceline in which the users can advertise their demand with the desired price to a group of sellers online. Then. Priceline will try to match the demand with the interested sellers who provide the desired price offering by the user. The company will gain the commission via the fulfilled transaction online. Distributor — is an intermediary operation that connects many product manufacturers with volume and retail buyers. A broker facilitates business transactions between franchised distributors and their trading partners.

Auction broker conducts auctions for either individuals or merchants to get the highest bidder in the market. Reverse auctions are a common variant which the buyer sourcing items via contact to get the lowest price seller in the market. Reverse auction helps the buyer to decrease the price; as the sellers compete to offer the best price or deal whilst meeting the expectation stated in the contract. Auction broker charges the seller a listing fee according to the value of the transaction.

Transaction broker provides a third-party payment mechanism via an online platform for buyers and sellers to facilitate a transaction. For instance, fsbohouse.com offers an online platform for sellers or buyers to facilitate the property deal with lower commission than traditional real estate agents. Distributor network with many product manufacturers and retail buyers often need the broker to make the deal between them. For instance, the broker facilitates business transactions between franchised distributors and their trading partners.

Bounty broker is given a prize for searching the difficult to find item, person, idea. Search agent performs the searching activity for information such as the price and availability for a good or service specified by the buyer. Web crawlers also known as spiders, crawlers, are programs that browse through the Internet using an algorithm to index content systematically. The market for web crawling service is mainly driven by the growing demand for business intelligence. It provides collective information, and the general market trends enable organizations to gain a competitive edge over competitors. All search brokers often reward with a flat fee or a percentage of rewards from the found items.

Licensing

Licensing content, product, technology can be a great source of revenue for a startup business. This may be done either by charging the licensors (users) for a flat or variable fee. Charging a fee on the licensed product is common in non-competitive business line, and for the non-sales purpose. Here, the licensor is an end user. Therefore, it is more reasonable to charge the licensor with either a fixed or used fee. If your licensor is in the same line of business and uses the products for sales, then charging a percentage of the revenue is a better approach. This way, the licensee (owner) makes recurring revenues each time their licensed product is sold by a licensor.

Licensing is a money-making, especially in software development and content creation business. Identifying the right revenue model, and picking the target segment of the customer is important in establishing a sustainable business model.

Licensing provides the opportunity for businesses to expand without using their own resources by venturing into non-related industry business. Licensee may collaborate with another industry partner to build sophisticated products and services. For instance, Google offers its Google map service with Uber to develop a navigation system for the ride-hailing application.

Licensing is not ideal for every business and could be detrimental if not deployed strategically. A general rule of thumb is not to license the direct competitor. Licensing would let a weaker rival offers a product as well as yours, or a stronger competitor to overcome the shortcoming. The ideal licensing model is where your product forms a vital component, for the non-competitor in a different industry. Uber leveraging on Google Maps is the mutual benefit example of a licensing model. Other common licensing models, including music for use in an event, commercial space, theatre, movie and the patents in the electronic devices. For instance, Google and Android phone manufacturer have cross-licensing agreements to utilize each other's patents in a non- competitive position to create a more customer-centric mobile device.

Advertising

An advertising revenue model is a business approach that focuses on advertising as a major source of income. This revenue model is important in traditional broadcast, print media and modern online media. Media company gains income from advertising, customer subscriptions or both.

Traditional media like TV, radio, along with newspapers and magazines entertain or inform audiences or readers. TV and radio have traditionally been mainly advertising-supported. While networks and satellite TV stations earn part of revenue via viewer subscriptions, they earn most of their revenue from advertisers trying to appeal against the audiences. Similarly, magazines and newspapers charge subscription or purchase fees, but advertisers also pay to place ads within these print media. Modern entrepreneurs should focus on online media for the advertising revenue model.

    The emergence of the Internet in the mid-1990s has disrupted the advertising revenue model. Newspaper's publisher, for instance, tried to shift for online content and reduced publication of hard copy. Modern media companies have established thousands of media websites, which offer free content for users. With the large user base, they attract businesses to advertise banner ads and advertorial ad spaces on their website. Traditional newspapers have shifted online with free content, but many are trying to figure out how to combine ad revenue with subscription fees.

The advantage of an advertising revenue model is that if you have a large base of viewers or subscribers, you can easily find companies that want to pay for advertisement. The ad-supported model is workable when you can provide the details of the niche of audiences to the businesses. When you operate on the ad-supported model without the subscription, you can easily attract users with free content. Both traditional and online media have long given away free content to the mass or target viewers, to drive up their reputation by increasing the circulation of free content, and subsequently the ramp up advertising revenue.

The major disadvantage of 100% advertising revenue model is the inherent lack of diversification of income. During the economic downturn, most advertisers might cut their budgets on the advertisement, which reduce the revenue of the advertisers without subscription revenue. Besides that, costs on the website, publication and other overhead expenses are big of sustaining the business operation. Thus, a mixture of free and paid content can help to cover costs and entice viewers. The subscription revenue might not be substantial, but it helps offset costs and allow advertising revenue to build.

Revenue Management

The revenue management process begins with the data collection to create a model with a forecasting power. With the forecasting tool, entrepreneurs can derive the actionable insights from the data. They must also analyze the inventories, sales, prices, the volume of sales, customer information and other relevant data for market segmentation. It is used for market-based pricing and revenue maximization. For instance, Airlines charge differently for both business and economy class passengers, off-peak and peak season passengers, and different pricing via multiple channels such as online platform, travel agencies, and other ticket agents.

Revenue management requires accurate forecasting on demand, price, and inventory. The revenue depends critically on the quality and accuracy of these forecasts. Thus, it is necessary to allocate resources and time to develop the right model with forecasting capabilities. Both Qualitative and Quantitative methods often complement each other shortcomings in forecasting. The qualitative method allows one to use the judgment and subjective knowledge in forecasting. One can make good use of a qualitative method, especially when there is no historical data for the new product. The Quantitative model depends on previous data and tries to model a scenario based on the variables in the data set. An entrepreneur can do policy making using a predictive model such as machine learning application.

It explains past behavior well, but forecasting is only accurate as long as the existing collected data (independent variables) can explain the real-life condition of the market to give correct prediction (dependent variable).

4 ways to increase revenues
Acquiring the new customer

　　Acquiring the new customers means you're trying to bring more customers to your business. This is the most effective approach: as the number of customers grew, more patronage to business will generate more sales. You may need to segment, target and position your customers based on their lifestyles, buying habit to provide a solution of their concern issues. As customer habits are changing constantly, you should be reviewing the user profiles consistently, to ensure your business can detect any new trends from consumer purchase record.

There are a number of non-competitive complementary businesses. These related businesses have broad customer bases of whom may also be the ideal customers for your company. By connecting and building mutually benefits partnership via referrals program, you greatly expanding customer base and creating another reliable source of income, to complement with existing sales channel.

Customers like special promotion or deal because it makes them feel like they're getting in on something worth more than the actual value. It also creates a sense of urgency, customers tend to purchase the promotional items as quickly as possible before the end of sales. The most rewarding sales campaigns don't just capture the attention of the customers, but they inspire it sharing as well. Social media channels are an ideal channel for free advertising, building the brand and reputation online. When users share your sales campaign, their immediate family and friends are more likely to be influenced. Because it's coming from someone they familiar, and trust to have their best interest in mind, rather than an advertisement from an unknown company.

A commercial website is another important tool for a business to get new customers. A website contains free, useful information on products or services for visitors. Besides that, it's imperative that the website comes with dedicated lead generation pages. Other than that, it must get the contact information and sales conversion page. These can be content pages that customers connect to via email, promotion webpage, or marketing campaigns. Be sure that they have free giveaways, click to action (CTA) buttons, consultation forms, or whatever method to get customers' information. Customer testimonials, reviews, and recommendations are some of the most powerful tools to entice online customers. Customers don't actually connect directly with a company; they connect with the people that associate with it. Give your customers the freedom to comment on your website, to remind they aren't just buying a "product," they are buying the access to a community of like-minded people whom they can interact with each other. Any form of positive social proof can increase the conversion rate. It addressing some of the doubt that may be holding the potential customers back, as they tend to make purchase decisions influenced by favorable comments from the existing customers.

Retaining existing customer

    Keeping the existing customer means encouraging existing customers to purchase from you more often. For example, if your customers purchase once a month, convincing them to buy once a week will increase sales significantly. The more frequently they purchase, the higher income your business will bring in, assuming the average transaction value stays the same.

The good customer relationship is the best way to keep existing customers. Reward them with exclusive benefits as an appreciation for their patronage. For instance, as customers order their fourth product from your company. A week later, they receive a free cash voucher with a handwritten note thanking them for the purchase. This type of unexpected appreciation helps to improve overall customer satisfaction and offsetting the tiny cost of gifts. Genuinely care about your customers! It doesn't mean doing superficial things like sending little gifts, smiling at your meetings, but doing a study to learn more about new technologies or options that might benefit them in the long run. Be proactive to customers' needs, and responsive in gathering and engaging with the feedback is important to keep them happy.

Using the data of purchased history or browsed record on the website, entrepreneurs can design the specific content and product recommendations in marketing campaigns. They may test incentives (discount, promotion) and other non-incentive factors (content of marketing material) to create the most effective way enticing the repeat customer. Top eCommerce company often emphasize the limited-time promotion. The visitors must complete the purchase quickly to get the special deal. In addition, you can add the coupon, gift card to the shopper's cart automatically, and highlight the deal during the checkout process. This promotion kills two birds with one stone: the limited-time deal increases the conversion rate in the most recent period, and the gift card brings customers back to the website to make another repeat purchase.

A VIP program takes loyalty points to the next level by giving customers both elevated status and exclusive offers. They enjoy more rewards as they shop. With the reward program, customers purchase repeatedly from the same seller to get more benefits on the money they spent. Align expectations with your customers regularly. Keep in mind that be transparent and honest about what you inform the existing customers. Over-promising and under-delivering is the easiest way to lose trustworthiness. Gaining customer trust goes a long way towards getting consumers to like your brand — so keep everything from product descriptions to promotional activities as accurate as possible similar to the feature and quality of the actual products or services.

Increasing the transaction value

Increasing the transaction value means you're trying to entice each customer to purchase more in a transaction. It typically does this through a process called upselling or cross-selling. Cross-selling is a selling technique that recommends complementary products that satisfy the unfulfilled needs of the main item. For example, a mouse could be cross-sold to a customer purchasing a personal computer. Often, cross-selling offers consumers the products they would have bought to generate sales at the right time.

Cross-selling is common to every type of business. For instance, banks and insurance agencies often use cross-selling to increase the value of transaction. Debit cards, credit cards, investment funds, and other financial products are cross-sold to depositors opening a savings account. Insurance agencies suggest life insurance to customers buying a medical card, saving plan. By showing the breadth of a catalog to customers, they are likely to purchase more than intended. E-Commerce website uses the cross-selling technique in sales campaigns, on product pages, and during the checkout process. It is an effective tactic for generating higher sales from a single transaction. Sellers can cross-selling with the product catalogs, and diversifying the existing product range. This will be further earning consumer's confidence to label the seller as the complete solution provider for the type of products.

Other than that, up-selling is another effective way to increase average transaction value. Selling the premium, upgraded products or more quantity of the same products to the customer is a direct way to make more sales. Avoid recommending a product or service that is significantly more expensive than the product being purchased. Thus, you may offer the products based on the customer spending power by using the average transaction value, income level, and education, etc. For a business-to-business customer, focus on business size and the number of employees. Never hard sell to customers, focus on their actual needs, and explain how the value-added offer will help them meet those needs. As a rule of thumb, if you cannot justify how the additional purchase will benefit the customer's overall goals, then it's not an upsell even worth considering. Not everyone is a viable customer for an upsell, and you should never, ever hard sell additional products or services to a customer who doesn't really need them. For example, if you're considering pitching the premium enterprise resource planning software to a small business owner, but doesn't fit directly into his long-term plan, you shouldn't force it. If you try to sell the product that cannot deliver any positive result to the customer, you not only losing the trust of the customer and potential risk of losing his business altogether.

When meeting with customers, focus on their most concern issues, offer a solution and upsell to them, so business misses no opportunity to create sales. Always promote an upgrade within the context of an idea related to customers' needs. If you see an opportunity to help a customer increases the leads from social platform marketing, come up with a solid plan to help him achieve it. Don't just promote the products for the sake of getting your sales–provide an actionable plan to generate quality leads on the social platform for the customer. Commit to bringing real values to the customers right from day one — and that the products or services can live up with the expectation to deliver the tangible results.

Compare side-by-side the features of your products so that the customer can see the benefit of the premium version. When you're proposing an upsell, it's especially important to provide transparent pricing information. Give your customers a complete pricing breakdown and explain the benefit and cost involved. If a customer understands the value of money spent, they'll feel more confident about investing the money on it.

Offer the discounted price, bundle in quantities, purchase with purchase, or personalized discount to encourage the customer to make an immediate purchase decision. Successful in-person upselling might require training for the techniques. Understanding how to upsell effectively can generate additional income, but doing it the wrong could turn away existing business.

Optimizing prices

Optimizing prices mean you'll gain more money from every transaction of your business. A positive relationship does not exist between a company's total revenue and the prices of its products or services. Higher prices do not always lead to better sales for a business. When prices change, a business owner must consider elasticity to gauge the actual impact on the total revenues. Therefore, a change in price can either be positive or negative to the sales.

The elasticity of demand means the interaction between the demand of the products and its price. When a company raises its prices, the demand from the customers may change in response with a higher price. Therefore, the change in total revenues must consider from both price and demand. A hike in price does not guarantee to result in an increased sale. However, when a company plans to reduce prices, the company must gain additional sales, particularly if the decrease in price is substantial enough to gain huge market share. Here, the surge in the customers' demand may offset the immediate decrease in an average transaction resulting from the cheaper prices.

To forecast the effect of prices will have on revenue, a company must conduct a research to gauge its impact. By determining the customer's willingness to pay at the micro-level (based on individual data), a company can predict more accurately the actual impact of the price change on the total sales. The main priority when forecasting the net effect of price changes on revenues is the elasticity of demand. For the inelastic market, the customer is price insensitive as the demand does not change with price. In simpler words, the customer will buy the same quantity regardless of price. In an elastic market, the customer is price sensitive since the changes in price results in the significant drop in demand. Therefore, the price surge in the inelastic condition would lead to increased sales. However, a price hike in the elastic market would lead to decreased revenues.

Chapter 7- Cost
Financial Cost

Cost is the money needed in a process of generating sales via product/service. An entrepreneur needs to understand the various expenses incurred in the business. Cost structures differ from one company to another. Therefore, the expense accounts appearing on a financial statement depend on the cost objects, such as a product, service, project, customer, or business activity. Even within a company, cost structure may vary between product lines, divisions or business units, due to the business activity, it performs.

Financial costs are expenses that a company incurs via its operations. For instance, the cost of raw materials, semi-finished products, and finished goods along with administrative expenses, such as rent, salaries, insurance, and utilities.

Organization record accounting costs in the statement of profit and loss (P/L).

Operating expenses (OPEX)

Operating expenses are the costs for a company to run its business operations. Examples include rent, utilities, salaries, costs on sales, general, & administrative (SG&A), research & development, tax; etc. Operational expenses take up the large portion of a company's costs. Entrepreneurs actively look for the measure to reduce operating expenses without causing a significant drop in quality or production of output. In contrast to capital expenditures, operating costs are tax-deductible in the year incurred.

Capital Expenditures (CAPEX)

Capital expenditures are the costs that companies purchase fixed assets for utilizing for more than a year. For example, a company might have capital expenditures on the assets to get more sales. Fixed assets categorized as non-current assets (building, machine, equipment, vehicles, etc.) from an accounting standpoint as they are not likely to convert into cash in the first year. It normally charges to expense throughout the functional life of the asset, using depreciation.

Capital expenditures might include big-ticket items such as the machine, equipment, vehicle, building (retail store, factory, office), building renovation (expansion, upgrade), hardware (computers, furniture). The industry that a company ventured in largely determines the nature of its capital expenditures. A business should at least maintain the previous level of capital expenditures. Otherwise, it will lead to a decline in business if the reinvestment is inadequate in the organization. A business should increase capital expenditure to ramp-up production if the management foresees the expansion of the business.

Economic Cost

Variable cost and fixed cost are the two main costs in the economy. A company's total cost is the sum of the fixed costs and variable costs. Variable costs fluctuate with the output produced. Fixed costs stay the same, no matter how much output produced.

Fixed Costs

Fixed costs incurred on the regular interval as long as the business thrives. It is most likely maintaining at the same rate in the stipulated period. Examples of fixed costs are overhead costs such as monthly rentals, interest expenses, taxes, amortization, depreciation of fixed assets.

Certain types of businesses have been high fixed costs, because of the leasing cost on equipment or commercial space. For example, a printing service has substantial costs on the printer, rental of space regardless the volume of business has. However, once those fixed costs reach the breakeven point, it is fairly easy to generate profits from then on due to low variable costs.

Variable Costs

Variable costs are expenses that change with the volume of production. Examples of variable costs are the cost that involves directly in the production of goods & services. For instance, direct material cost, labor costs, bonuses, commissions, utilities, and marketing expenses.

A company that aims to increase its profit by cutting costs may need to focus on variable costs for raw materials, direct labor, and advertising. However, the cost-cutting initiatives must be optimized, so it doesn't affect product or service quality, as this would have a negative impact on sales. By reducing the variable costs, a business increases its gross profit margin and eventually leads to a profit-making position easily.

Sunk Cost

Sunk cost is also known as embedded cost, past cost, prior year cost, stranded cost, sunk capital, or retrospective cost. A sunk cost is a cost that has already incurred and cannot be recovered. Thus, Sunk costs are an independent event and should not consider when making future investment or project.
To make an informed decision, the business owners only considers the costs and revenues that will fluctuate because of the decision; they do not consider sunk costs. For example, A manufacturing firm may have several sunk costs, such as the cost of equipment, heavy machinery, and the lease cost of a factory. It should exclude these costs when making future investment or project. All sunk costs are fixed costs. However, not all fixed-costs are sunk costs.

Opportunity Cost

Opportunity cost represents the benefits business misses out on when choosing one option over another. While financial reports do not show opportunity cost, entrepreneurs can use it to make informed decisions when they have multiple choices in hands.

When assessing the profitability of investments or projects, businesses pick for the best option that is likely to generate the greatest return from all available options. However, businesses must also consider the opportunity cost of other available alternatives. Assume that, given a capital for investment, a business must choose between investing funds in a new business or using it to purchase new machinery. No matter which option the business chooses, the potential profit it gives up on the abandon option is the opportunity cost.

The formula for Calculating Opportunity Cost

Opportunity cost is the difference between the expected returns of each option: Opportunity cost = return of abandon option - the return of the chosen option. For example, an entrepreneur has two investment opportunities.

Option 1 Invest in the stock market with 0%-10% return, since the value of an investment depends on its market value. Option 2 Reinvest in newer equipment with 8% return. It will enhance the operating efficiency and revenues.

	Oppurtunity cost =	Option not chosen Equipment	Option chosen Stock Market
WORST CASE	8.0%	8%	0%
	7.0%	8%	1%
	6.0%	8%	2%
	5.0%	8%	3%
	4.0%	8%	4%
	3.0%	8%	5%
	2.0%	8%	6%
	1.0%	8%	7%
	0.0%	8%	8%
	-1.0%	8%	9%
BEST CASE	-2.0%	8%	10%

Scenario 1
Risk-taking business owner chooses investment in stock market.

The worst case is 8% of opportunity cost when the equity value wipes out completely, with less 8% of the return when investing in equity. The best cast is -2% of opportunity cost when the equity value gains 10%, with an additional 2% to return when investing in equity.

Upside potential is 2%; downside potential is 8%.

	Oppurtunity cost =	Option not chosen Stock Market	Option chosen Equipment
BEST CASE	-8.0%	0%	8%
	-7.0%	1%	8%
	-6.0%	2%	8%
	-5.0%	3%	8%
	-4.0%	4%	8%
	-3.0%	5%	8%
	-2.0%	6%	8%
	-1.0%	7%	8%
	0.0%	8%	8%
	1.0%	9%	8%
WORST CASE	2.0%	10%	8%

Scenario 2

Risk-averse business owner chooses the investment on equipment.

The worst case is 2% of opportunity cost when the equity earns the full expected return of 10%, with 2% less of return when investing in equipment.

The best cast -8% of opportunity cost when the equity value wipes out completely, an additional 8% of return when investing in equipment.
Upside potential is 8%, downside potential is 2%.

It is important to compare investment options with risk consideration. It is a safer choice in scenario 2 since the reward is greater (8%) than risk (2%). On the other hands, scenario 1 is the riskier option since the risk (8%) is higher than reward (2%). Thus, scenario 2 is a better choice of investment with less opportunity cost and higher return.

Opportunity cost analysis plays an important role in deciding the capital structure of the business. Funding via both equity and debt require an expense. For debt, interest payment is the cost of funding to compensate lenders. For equity, the return or dividends are the cost of funding to compensate the risk shareholders. Each option also bears an opportunity cost. Therefore, entrepreneurs must choose the right mix of capital structure. They need to optimize the capital structure by considering risk and reward of all options to maximize the value of the company.

Economies of Scale

The economy of scale is the cost-benefit that a company gains with an increased quantity of a specific good or service. The quantity of output and the fixed costs are in an inverse relationship. Put simply, as the number of goods and services increase, marginal cost will drop.

For example, consider a cup maker. Each cup produced requires $0.50 of porcelain. The factory incurs $200 dollars of fixed costs every month. If the factory makes 100 cups, then each cup incurs $2.00 ($200/100unit) of fixed costs. Therefore, the total cost per cup, including the porcelain, would be $2.50 ($2.50= $0.50+ ($200/100units)).

However, if the factory increased the production unit to 200 cups per month, then each cup would cost only $1.00 ($200/200units) of fixed cost. This happens because the fixed-costs shared between more units of output. The total cost per cup would then drop to $1.50 ($1.50 = $0.50+ ($200/200units)). Therefore, marginal cost reduces $1.00 when the 100 unit increases to 200 units of production. In this situation, increasing production volume causes the total cost decreases significantly.

When the fixed costs covered, the marginal cost per unit goes down. At lower marginal costs, additional units represent increasing profit margins. It gives price competitiveness for a seller offers an item in bulk. Warehouse retailers (Walmart, Costco, Tesco) leverage on the economy of scale by buying in bulk and packaging in a smaller unit for sale.

Although an economy of scale may seem beneficial to a company, it has limitations. Marginal costs never decrease indefinitely. At some point, operations become too big to keep experiencing economies of scale. This typically follows the law of diminishing returns where a further increase in output will cause an even greater increase in average total cost. This is the concept of diseconomies of scale. It forces companies to innovate business ideas, improve working capital or optimizing the level of production to remain competitive.

Economies of Scope

The economy of scope means the average total cost of a company's production decreases when there is a variation of goods made. The economy of scope provides the cost benefit to a company. This happens when it made a range of products while focusing on its related business's core competencies. One easy way to think about the economy of scope is to imagine that it's cheaper to manufacture two products by sharing the same resources.

    Economies of scope are important for the company, especially for a large corporation, and it can go about achieving the aim in three main ways. The economies of scope can be attained by improving internal efficiency via related diversification. For instance, Procter and Gamble manufacture the range of hygienic products under the different brand name using existing production line and business support unit.

    Merger and acquisition deals are another way to achieve economies of scope. Two companies with a similar line of business may merge with each other to produce goods or services using the same resources. It makes the simultaneous manufacturing of different products more cost-effective than manufacturing them on their own. For example, Google acquired Android, with joint efforts. They launch the Android operating system for handheld devices successfully within a few years with only a fraction of cost. Today, Android has become the duopoly player of the mobile OS in par with Apple OS, defeating competitors like BlackBerry, Symbian, BlackBerry, and even Windows phone platform.

Finally, a company may achieve economies of scope via vertical integration by the joint utilization of inputs and leads to reductions in unit costs. Two ways of integration: backward integration and forward integration. A company acquires the supply chain is practicing backward integration. A company that expands toward the front into distribution and point of sale is practicing forward integration. Apple Inc. is one of the best-known companies for vertical integration. Apple manufactures its custom A-series chips, touch ID fingerprint sensor, LCD and OLED screen using its own manufacturing plant. The Apple premium reseller model, where the company's products sell at the company-licensed distributor, this allows the business to control the distribution of the product to the end user.

COMPARISON	ECONOMIES OF SCALE	ECONOMIES OF SCOPE
Meaning	Economies of scale gains cost advantage due to the increasing number of output produced, using common resources	Economies of scope refers to savings in cost due to the production of multiple products, using common resources
Resources	Large quantities of similar raw materials using common resources	Varieties of raw materials using common resources
Task Complexity	Relatively simple planning	More complex scheduling and planning
Cost Reduction	Average total cost of one product	Average total cost of multiple products
Cost Advantage	Due to volume	Due to variation
Production	Fixed production line	Flexible production line
Product line	Standardization of product	Diversification product

Cost Control & Performance Management

Cost control by the management means a search for better and more economical ways of performing an activity in an organization. Cost control is the prevention of waste of resources within the organization. It is the practice of identifying and reducing business expenses to increase profits. It is also an important factor for maintaining and growing profitability. Businesses use outsourcing to control costs because many businesses find it cheaper to pay a third party to perform certain non-core or peripheral tasks rather than accomplish everything on their own. Cost controls rely on the past trend to make an informed decision on the present situation. Cost control applies to procedures, processes or activities, which have common standards. It seeks to attain the lowest cost optimizing the use of resources.

Entrepreneurs need to review both fixed and variable costs and try to reduce the expenses. Latter costs should be the focus since it changes with the volume of sales. The cost of goods sold (COGS) is a variable cost that can optimize significantly. It can be optimized by searching for suppliers to source items at more competitive prices. Bargaining with an existing supplier to get better deals in terms of lower unit cost, quantity discount, payment terms are among the ways to reduce COGS. It is difficult to reduce fixed costs, such as the salary, lease payment, utility because they usually fix in the stipulated period to sustain the business operation.

Budgetary control

    A budget is the prospect of financial statements such as P&L, cash flow, balance sheet. Budgeting refers to the formulation of the plan in numerical terms for a financial year. Budgetary cost control is the control activity that uses the budget to control cost. A variance is defined as the difference between budgeted amount and actual results. Entrepreneurs use the variance to identify critical areas that need a change. They must emphasize the largest dollar variance on company results. If the actual cost is more than the budget, they can exercise the control measure to reduce the cost to the budgeted amount or amend with a new reasonable budget plan. On the other hands, if expenses less than the budget without compromising the quality of the output, they must implement good practice within the organization. Some businesses analyze percentage variances and take-action on those actual costs that have the largest percentage variance from the budgeted costs.

Horizontal analysis

Horizontal analysis or trend analysis is a financial statement analysis technique that shows differences in the financial statement items with at least two periods of comparison. It is an effective tool to examine the trend. Typically, the comparison is made between two or more periods. The analysis is conducted by comparing the absolute monetary value items in the financial statements. For example, entrepreneurs can compare cash in hand in the current to other accounting periods. Another method is via the percentage variance using the earliest period as the base period to compare with a later period on the item of the financial statements. The changes can be shown both in dollars and percentage. They can conduct the horizontal analysis for cash flow, income statement, balance sheet. This method is helpful in identifying the items which are changing the most. The difference of amount and percentage term computed by using the following formulas:

Amount Difference:
The variance of an amount: Value of current period-Value of the base period

Percentage variance: Variance of amount/ Value of base period X 100

The horizontal analysis allows a company owner to see what has been driving a company's financial performance. It helps to spot the seasonal trend over the period of comparison. It enables the business owner to assess relative changes in different line items over the period of comparison. By looking at the income statement, entrepreneurs can examine the revenue and costs on what has been driving a company's financial performance, particularly profitability.

For cash flow trend analysis, the healthy cash flow trend shows a business is in a stable position to fulfill the business obligations. While a business can borrow money to get through the shortfall of cash to prevent defaults or foreclosures. Cash flow differs from the actual cash position. Having cash is important while positive cash flow shows the capability to generate and use cash.

Horizontal analysis can be linked to the key performance index (KPI) such as inventory turnover, profit margin. It can detect emerging issues and strengths of the business. For example, net profit may have been surging because the falling cost of goods sold, or because of the growing revenues. Other KPI, like the cash flow-to-debt ratio and the interest coverage ratio, shows the ability of a company to service its debt with cash. Horizontal analysis is also an easier approach to compare growth rates and profitability between different companies.

Vertical analysis
Vertical analysis is the proportional analysis of a financial statement. This analysis converted each item on a financial statement into a percentage of the base item. This means that all items on an

income statement converted into a percentage of gross sales, while every item on a balance sheet calculated as a percentage of total assets.

The most common application of vertical analysis is within a financial statement for a single time period. It enables entrepreneurs to see the relative proportion's comparison with the percentage (as the similar benchmark). In an income statement, every item is stated as a percentage of gross sales. It is also suitable for timeline analysis, to observe the difference in accounts, for two- or more-year comparison. For example, if the cost of goods sold has a history of being 40% of sales in the past two years, then a new percentage of 48% of the most recent year shows the significant rise of cost, the business owner may need to reexamine the efficiency of the procurement process, or seeks the alternative suppliers for better deals.

For the balance sheet, every item is converted as a percentage of total assets. This analysis can examine the capital structure. It shows the right mix of equity and debt in comparison with total assets. For an example, if the total asset is $1000,000, account payable is $100,000 or 10% of the total assets. The account receivable is $ 150,000 or 15% of total assets. The current assets (account receivable) are higher than current liabilities (account payable). Therefore, the working capital is sufficient to meet the short-term obligations.

Entrepreneurs can compare the percentage with previous year figure. They can observe the trends and have a better understanding of the financial position of their company. If the equity is shrinking, while the asset is rising. It indicated the invested asset may not be effective in generating enough revenues, creating value for shareholders. Entrepreneurs must develop new strategies to change operation activity using the asset efficiently. Such period to period comparisons enabled entrepreneurs to identify issues and underlying causes of it. They may take the right action to solve the problem instantly.

www.ingramcontent.com/pod-product-compliance
Lightning Source LLC
Chambersburg PA
CBHW031418210526
45464CB00005B/1946